musée de l'Orangerie

text by Jean-Noël von der Weid

art lys : VISIT GUIDE

Summary

06   The Sistine Chapel
of Impressionism

08   "My heart will belong
to Giverny forever …"

10   The Waterlilies • room 1 - room 2

30   The Walter-Guillaume Collection

▲   page 10

▲   page 20

▲   page 32

▲   page 46

▲ page 54

▲ page 66

▲ page 72

▲ page 76

The Sistine Chapel of Impressionism

The Orangerie was built in the second half of the 16th century on the site of Paris' first bastion of the three walls surrounding Paris, known as the Fossé Jaunes *(Yellow Trenches)*, referring to the color of the earth. This bastion within the Tuileries then became the first bastion, military zone was transformed into a green area: its military role, exclusive under Henry III and Henry IV, cohabited with the Tuileries gardens under Louis XIII. In 1668, the 'decorative' role finally won over with the works of André Le Nôtre, Louis XIV's gardener and Controller of Royal Buildings, who integrated the bastion into his new plan for the Tuileries Chateau gardens. Parisians rapidly came to enjoy shady walks overlooking the Seine, with splendid views of the surrounding countryside.

In 1852, the Orangerie Museum took as its home this former orangery, where, as its name indicates, the Tuileries grew its own fruit trees. The building resembled a long stone box, with glass panels on the south side where the Seine flows, and bricked over to the north on the garden side. This discreet style remains in harmony with the classicism of the Place de la Concorde and the Tuileries Palace (that no longer exists).

Under the Third Republic (1870-1940), the building was used both as a warehouse for military equipment and a venue for sports, musical and patriotic events, as well as industrial, canine and horticultural exhibits, and a few painting exhibits. In 1921, the Orangerie was handed over to the Beaux-Arts. In the meantime, in 1918, Claude

Monet had decided to donate two paintings to France, a decision that resulted in Monet planning the museum's interior layout and the installation of a grand series of *Waterlilies* on which he had been working since 1914, which installation would occur after his death (eight compositions consisting in 22 panels), all this thanks to the wise influence of Georges Clemenceau. Starting in 1958, a prestigious series of 19th and 20th century paintings collected by the art dealer, Paul Guillaume, and after his death, by his wife, Jean Walter, were donated to the Nation. It was agreed that the Orangerie Museum would house this collection. However, the works planned to host the collection disturbed the harmony Monet had sought by adding a first floor over the *Waterlilies*, and therefore a ceiling that barred natural and living light. The restructuring of the museum was planned at the beginning of the 1990s. The renovations, based on a detailed assessment of the specifics of the collections and intentions of their donors, lasted six years, from 2000 to 2006. The first floor was demolished and, in order to continue housing the Walter-Guillaume Collection, new areas were created on the lower floors under the Orangerie terrace, over a surface of more than 3,000 m². Depending on the rooms, artificial or natural light (through bay windows) illuminate works by Cézanne, Renoir, Matisse, Laurencin, Derain, Modigliani and Utrillo. As for the *Waterlilies*, they have found their natural light in the museum now referred to as the "Sistine Chapel of Impressionism".

▲ Outside view
of the Orangerie Museum
with Rodin sculptures
Paris, Orangerie Museum

▲ View of the Hall:
Orangerie Museum
Paris, Orangerie Museum

"My heart will belong to Giverny forever ..."

In 1883, Claude Monet (1840-1926) discovered Giverny, a town located at the frontier of Normandy, on the right bank of the Seine where it meets one of the Epte River branches, bordered by weeping willows and poplars. The artist, delighted with this location, only left it for brief periods and rented the "Maison du Pressoir", in which he moved with his spouse and children. Far from the bitter rivalries of the capital, juries and jealousy, he contemplated, studied and reinvented nature. It would be his only workshop. Monet became its owner seven years later and slowly transformed the house, passionate to the point of obsession with its plants and flowers. He joyfully created a flower garden with floral and tree species from Japan, and later a strange and tangled water garden, with black bamboo, ferns, bean trees and waterlilies. (He built a vast workshop in which he painted almost all his major *Waterlily* works.) This garden included a Japanese bridge that this "gardener-artist" completed with a structure to stimulate the growth of the wisteria. The garden was designed to encourage the lively intensity of colors, drawing the spectator's attention to their diversity, depth and shades. According to the artist, the garden was "pleasant and agreeable to the eyes, and also provided subjects to be painted". Monet never ceased caring for it. Even during his absences, whether long or short, his letters always included multiple recommendations.

▼▼ Claude Monet 's garden
at Giverny.
Waterlily Pond

◄ Monet touching up
the edge of a painting
in his workshop in 1920

▲
Claude Monet near
the Waterlily pond

WATERLILIES, OR THE UNIVERSE REFLECTED IN WATER

▶ Inspired by the water garden and waterlily pond in his Giverny home, between 1895 and his death in 1926, Claude Monet painted the gigantic *Waterlilies* series (more than two hundred and fifty paintings), in addition to approximately forty large "panels". In their final version, the Orangerie's *Waterlilies* include eight compositions divided into twenty-two panels that are exhibited in two rooms. Shortly after the Armistice in 1918, Claude Monet offered Georges Clemenceau, an old friend who was the current head of the government, to donate to France two panels on the waterlily theme. After lengthy negotiations, two rooms in the Orangerie of the Tuileries laid out in a rotunda, pursuant to the artist's wishes, were selected to house the *Waterlilies*. Monet, whose health and sight were weakening, had not realized the immensity of his undertaking. His spouse, eldest son, Jean, and close friends (Mallarmé, Pissarro, Degas and Renoir) successively died during this period. Supported by Clemenceau, the painter retrieved his "real vision" after a cataract operation in 1923 and finally returned to work, completing it in April 1926. The installation of the works followed shortly after the painter's death: the inauguration took place on May 17, 1927. Innovative and almost abstract, these are the last works of Claude Monet, the former head of the Impressionist movement.

◀ Room 1, Waterlilies
Paris,
Orangerie Museum

◀ **Claude Monet**
(1840-1926)
Waterlilies, a water study:
Setting Sun
Paris, Orangerie Museum

▲ Waterlilies Room 1

Claude Monet
(1840-1926)
Waterlilies, a water study:
Clouds

Claude Monet
(1840-1926)
Waterlilies, a water study:
Green Reflection

Claude Monet
(1840-1926)
Waterlilies, a water study:
Morning No. 1

THE WATERLILIES: MISUNDERSTANDING AND ENTHUSIASM

▶ At first, the *Waterlilies* drew less enthusiasm than misunderstanding. While some considered the work to be purely decorative, others were troubled by the absence of markers and boundaries. A critic evoked the physical malaise these aquatic landscapes caused. In 1932, another, André Lhote, wrote: "For an artist, light only exists in color ... Simply see the artist's attraction for this phenomenon at the Orangerie: it has caused Claude Monet to commit plastic suicide. The Ophelia of painting, his soul wanders without glory in the shroud of waterlilies." Georges Clemenceau deeply admired the works of Monet, long before American artists of the 1950s, like Pollock or Rothko, claimed inspiration from this artist. He saw in the *Waterlilies* an "inexpressible storm where, through the painter's magic, our eye is overcome by its confrontation with the universe". Marcel Proust, tied to Monet by numerous affinities, treated the masterpiece with finesse: "Here and there, on the surface, like a strawberry, a waterlily reddens: a scarlet heart and white edges. Further on, the flowers grow in numbers and are paler, rougher, grainier, more crinkled and hazardly dispersed in mounds so graciously that you would think they are floating astray, like the melancholic farewells after a festivity, with bubbly roses forming unraveled garlands."

▲
▶ **Claude Monet**
(1840-1926)
Waterlilies, a water study:
Two Weeping Willows

Claude Monet
(1840-1926)
Waterlilies, a water study:
Morning No. 2

Claude Monet
(1840-1926)
Waterlilies, a water study:
Reflecting Trees

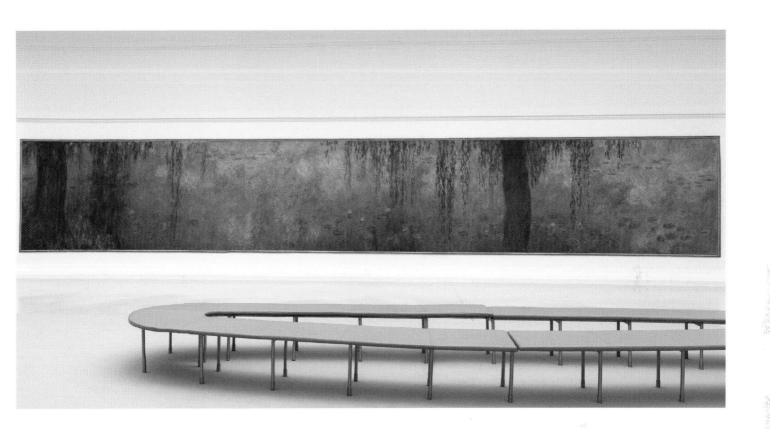

Claude Monet
(1840-1926)
Waterlilies, a water study: Morning
with Weeping Willows

THE WALTER-GUILLAUME COLLECTION

This collection owes its name to the modern art dealer, Paul Guillaume, and the architect and businessman, Jean Walter, both having died respectively in 1934 and 1957. Their common point: to have been married to Juliette Lacaze, otherwise known as the "Domenica", heir to the collection.

Paul Guillaume needed to work as a youth. Employed in an automobile garage, he discovered in a cargo of rubber, African sculptures that he displayed in a window. Guillaume Apollinaire, who is thought to have seen these works, became his mentor. The poet, Max Jacob, introduced him to Picasso, Picabia, De Chirico, Laurencin and Modigliani. He opened a small gallery in 1914, providing avant-garde artists supported by Apollinaire with a location to exhibit their works. After the war, Paul Guillaume moved his gallery to the opulent Rue de La Boétie where, supported by his shrewd wife, Domenica, he moved in political, cultural and social circles. Tasteful and energetic, he became a wise and shrewd art dealer, and also a true "player in the cultural world". His collection, which he attempted to broadly exhibit, never ceased growing and became one of the largest in Europe. Shortly before his death, Paul Guillaume considered making a donation to the Louvre. Remarried to Jean Walter, his wife, Domenica, who "tamed" the collection by removing avant-garde works, enriched it with works that were expensive to acquire. The Louvre lacking space, the collection moved to the Orangerie in the Tuileries which, at the time, depended on the Louvre. The collection only entered the Orangerie after Domenica's death in 1977. It has been exhibited here since 1984.

Reproduction of Domenica Walter's interior at 3 Rue du Cirque, circa 1965
Corner of the Library

◄ Kees Van Dongen
(1877-1968)
Portrait of Paul Guillaume
Circa 1930

◄ Dining Room in Paul
Guillaume's Apartment
Maquette by Rémi Munier

RENOIR AND CÉZANNE

Contemporaries and neighbors in southern France for some time, Pierre Auguste Renoir (1841-1919) and Paul Cézanne (1839-1906) differed in their esthetics and painting. Renoir, lyrical and light, played with Impressionist principles (light and pearly colors, effects of light) in his portraits that illustrate the freshness and elfin innocence of children, in his voluptuous nudes with their lavish curves, in his desire to paint "beings as lovely pieces of fruit"… At times, he blended these with scenery and the grandeur and illumination of nature. His works speak of harmony and serenity; their composition is peaceful and natural. Happiness in the present moment. He rejected introspection, explorations into character, dark and complicated subjects. For his part, Cézanne was a bizarre, bearded and gruff person (his fame came posthumously), who rapidly abandoned Impressionism. He progressively came to be one of the painters inspiring the emergence of modern art. Picasso said, "He is a father to all of us." A teasing point of light struggling between daylight and darkness; a sparkling shine of aquatic reflections, confronting sharp and intense forms; timid portraits that lack sensuality; rigid and frozen still lifes. Definitively living in Aix-en-Provence, his birth place, from 1862 onwards, Cézanne obsessively "pondered the landscape" (the Gulf of Marseille, Gardanne, Sainte-Victoire Mountain). Shortly before his death, he wrote in a letter: "I continue to study nature and I think I have made slow progress."

▲ Pierre Auguste Renoir
(1841-1919)
Female Bather with Long Hair
Circa 1895-1896

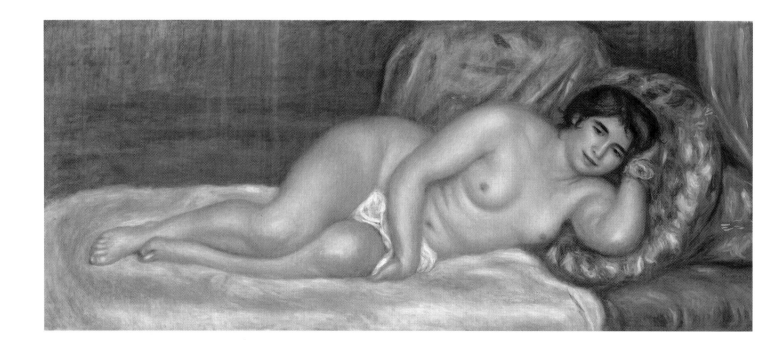

▲ Pierre Auguste Renoir
(1841-1919)
Lying Nude
(Gabrielle)
1906-1907

▲ Pierre Auguste Renoir
(1841-1919)
Nude Woman in a Landscape
1883

▲ Pierre Auguste Renoir
(1841-1919)
Seated Bather
Drying a Leg
Circa 1914

RENOIR AND MUSIC

Color, nuance, chromatism ... Painting and music have many points in common and can symbolize an era and even an esthetic movement: Renoir and Monet's Impressionism and that of Claude Debussy. Paintings bring life to musical instruments and spread the tranquil and serene atmosphere that surrounds a piano. A painter's opinion of a musician may even reveal certain esthetic trends. Renoir, for example: "Beethoven talks about himself indecently. He spares us neither his heartaches, nor his painful indigestion. I feel like saying to him: 'Why should I care that you are deaf! Degas painted at his best when he no longer could see! Mozart, who was much poorer than Beethoven, had the decency to hide his worries ...' Beethoven reveals less of himself with his noisy sobs."

▲ **Pierre Auguste Renoir**
(1841-1919)
Young Girls at the Piano
Circa 1892

▲ **Pierre Auguste Renoir**
(1841-1919)
Portrait of Two Girls
1890-1892

▲ Pierre Auguste Renoir
(1841-1919)
Claude Renoir as a Clown
1909

▲ Pierre Auguste Renoir
(1841-1919)
Claude Renoir Playing
Circa 1905

Pierre Auguste Renoir ▶
(1841-1919)
Gabrielle and Jean
Circa 1895-1896

▲ **Pierre Auguste Renoir**
(1841-1919)
Woman in a Hat
Circa 1915-1919?

▲ **Pierre Auguste Renoir**
(1841-1919)
Woman leaning on her Elbow
Circa 1917-1919

▲ **Pierre Auguste Renoir**
(1841-1919)
Gabrielle in the Garden
Circa 1905

◀◀ **Paul Cézanne** (1839-1906)
Portrait of Madame Cézanne
Circa 1890

◀ **Paul Cézanne** (1839-1906)
Portrait of the Artist's Son
1881-1882

▲ **Paul Cézanne** (1839-1906)
Fruits, Napkin
and Milk Jug
1880-1881

▲ **Paul Cézanne** (1839-1906)
Straw Vase, Sugar Bowl
and Apples
1890-1893

▲　Paul Cézanne (1839-1906)
Apples and Biscuits
1879-1880

Paul Cézanne (1839-1906)
Trees and Houses
1885-1886

▼ **Paul Cézanne** (1839-1906)
Park of Château Noir
1898-1900

▼ **Paul Cézanne** (1839-1906)
The Red Rock
Circa 1895

VISITING CÉZANNE

To meet Paul Cézanne, a singular artist, was a disconcerting experience. Unlike the legend, he was not a recluse, retired amongst his flowers at Giverny. Although he avoided certain indiscreet visitors, he constantly invited many of his intimate friends and confidants. Georges Clemenceau, Auguste Rodin, Jean Renoir, Octave Mirbeau and Paul Valéry, Victor Focillon, the engraver, Paul Durand-Ruel, the art dealer and collector and Georges Crès, the art editor, among others, kept him informed on news in the world of art. When Mary Cassatt, the American artist, first met him, she could not help but describe him in a letter: "When I saw him for the first time, I thought he was a type of brigand, with large and red protruding eyes, giving him a ferocious air, highlighted by his short and pointed beard, almost gray, and a manner of speaking that was so violent that plates literally resonated.

Afterwards, I discovered that his appearances had deceived me. Far from ferocious, he has the most delicate temperament possible, like a child ... I was surprised by his initial mannerisms. He scrapes his soup bowl, then raises it and lets the last drops fall onto his spoon... He eats off a knife, an instrument he firmly grasps at the beginning of each meal and that he only releases when he rises; it accompanies each gesture and each movement of his hand. However, despite his total disdain for good manners, he showed us courtesy unlike anyone else ..."

▲ Paul Cézanne (1839-1906)
The Boat and Bathers
Circa 1890

▲ Paul Cézanne (1839-1906)
A Luncheon on the Grass
1876-1877

▲ Paul Gauguin (1848-1903)
Landscape
1901

MODIGLIANI, ROUSSEAU AND LAURENCIN

The painter and sculptor, Amedeo Modigliani (1884-1920), arrived in Paris in 1906 where he discovered Montmartre le Bateau-Lavoir, buildings home to a group of artists in full creative development. There, he met Picasso and Apollinaire, then Utrillo and Soutine, who would become his most loyal friends, and lived the mad life of a bohemian. He died in Paris, the victim of alcohol and tuberculosis. In his paintings, this devilish artist adopted a sensible and disciplined style: the two hundred or so works from the period between 1914 and 1919 focus on a single theme, the human being (his life works include only four landscapes). Nudes, portraits of his wife, his friends and people unknown that he had simply met in passing ... The subjects seem disembodied; their expressions are melancholic, anxious and vulnerable; the lines are supple and elegant, sometimes strongly marked: prolonged necks, excessively thin hands, almond-shaped eyes, often without pupils, blank stares. However, when he painted people known to him, his precious nature hid or disguised the model's essential traits, those that would have revealed a true personality, without affecting, however, the charm, power and sensual heat of his art. While the naiveté and freshness of the self-taught Henri Rousseau, Le Douanier (1844-1920), call out to us - although they were mocked by the purists of the time - as they let us measure, touch and weigh what we see. We find allegorical and exotic landscapes (a series of "jungles"), scenes from daily life, portraits, still lifes ... As for the false naiveté of the stretched and suave feminine figures painted by Marie Laurencin (1885-1956), they are typically French: graceful.

◀ Amedeo Modigliani
(1884-1920)
The Young Apprentice
1918-1919

▼ Amedeo Modigliani
(1884-1920)
Woman with a Velvet Bow
Circa 1915

▼ Amedeo Modigliani
(1884-1920)
Paul Guillaume, Novo Pilota
1915

▼ Henri-Julien Félix Rousseau,
Le Douanier Rousseau
(1844-1910)
Old Junier's Cart
1908

ROUSSEAU'S SINCERITY

During Rousseau's life, critics showed little interest for his art, except to be negative. Certain writers, such as Alfred Jarry and Guillaume Apollinaire, were the first to admire him. In the words of Apollinaire in April 1911: "Few artists have been as broadly mocked during their life as Le Douanier and few men have faced mockery and rudeness with more calm. This courteous old man wanted to see, even in the mockery of the most malicious, an interest directed towards his work ... Le Douanier knew his strength ... He took his paintings to the ultimate, a very rare thing today. There are no mannerisms, process or system in his works. And that is where variety arises in his art."

▲ Henri-Julien Félix Rousseau,
Le Douanier Rousseau
(1844-1910)
The Chair Factory at Alfortville
Circa 1897? Circa 1906-1908?

▲ Henri-Julien Félix Rousseau,
Le Douanier Rousseau
(1844-1910)
Boat in the Storm
Circa 1899

▲ Henri-Julien Félix Rousseau,
Le Douanier Rousseau
(1844-1910)
The Wedding
Circa 1905

▲ **Marie Laurencin** (1885-1956)
Portrait of Mademoiselle Chanel
1923

▲ **Marie Laurencin** (1885-1956)
Spanish Dancers
Circa 1920-1921

MARIE LAURENCIN: A COMPLETE ARTIST

Marie Laurencin was the "Lady of Cubism", according to the famous expression of the poet, Guillaume Apollinaire, for whom she was a muse and partner from 1907 to 1912. She started painting in 1902 and was recognized as an artist in an environment dominated by men, who often thought women were "simple reflections of men" (Octave Mirbeau). Her works use soft and delicate colors. "I didn't like every color," she said. "So why use those I don't like? I simply left them aside. I only used blue, pink, green, white and black. With age, I came to accept yellow and red." Marie Laurencin insisted more on nuances than exuberance: her young girls are elegant and suave like angels. Their eyes are black, almond-shaped; the nose is gently outlined, the mouth firm and closed, the skin pale. The famous ballet director, Serge de Diaghilev, was the first to order ballet decors from her for *Les Biches (The Does)*, by the French composer, Francis Poulenc, an "erotic ballet" bringing together twenty young sylphs and three "solid good-looking guys in rowing suits". Marie Laurencin also illustrated numerous books.

▲ **Marie Laurencin** (1885-1956)
Portrait of Madame Paul Guillaume
Circa 1924

▲ **Marie Laurencin** (1885-1956)
The Does
1923

▲ Marie Laurencin (1885-1956)
Women with Dog
Circa 1923

PICASSO AND MATISSE

Without a doubt, no artist in the 20th century has caused as many comments, critiques or verbiage as the Spanish painter, drawer, engraver, sculptor, ceramist and writer, Pablo Picasso (1881-1973). This creator, considered universal, exercised an extraordinary power of fascination over his generation. Like Igor Stravinsky in music, his personality dominated the artistic life of the first half of the 20th century. Anything that Picasso touched, a human being, an acrobat, a common object, the works of another artist, he changed, twisted and unraveled, worried it or brought it peace, and made it into something that belonged only to him, something that could not exist without him - with breathtaking flamboyance.

While Picasso constantly questioned the universe with a violence that could also be gentle, Henri Matisse (1869-1954), a discreet and shy man, created works of peaceful beauty, where formal perfection blends in with fluid and luminous elegance. He ignored the convulsions of form and the jolts of the spirit. Less controversial than the impatient Spaniard, Matisse also used very distinct techniques (painting, sculpture, engraving, weaving, theater decors, illustrations, stained glass, cut paper ...) and deeply influenced 20th century art, without allowing his constantly changing work to be bound in by a passing esthetic school or movement (Cubism, Fauvism). With no visible difficulty, it seems he achieved the goal he had sought since 1908: "an art of balance, purity, tranquility".

◄ **Pablo Picasso** (1881-1973)
Nude on Red Background
1906

Pablo Picasso (1881-1973) ▷
The Embrace
1903

Pablo Picasso (1881-1973) ▽
Adolescents
1906

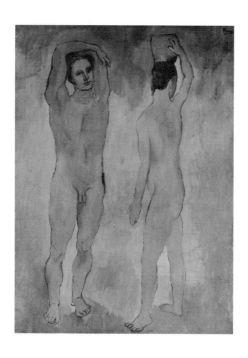

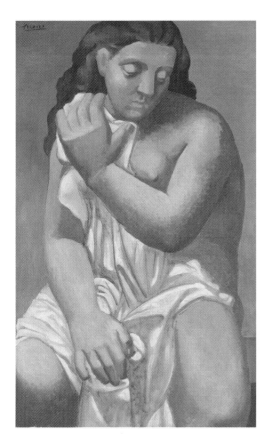

▲ **Pablo Picasso** (1881-1973)   ▲ **Pablo Picasso** (1881-1973)
Large Draped Nude   Large Bather
1920-1921   1921

PICASSO AND NATURE

All of Picasso's creations and natural metamorphoses have been the subject of endless guessing and comments. But the work of a genius cannot be simply limited by explanations. At most, one can express the admiration and feelings these works impose on us. Here is Picasso's perspective from the 1970s: "I don't want there to be three, four or a thousand ways of interpreting one of my paintings. I want there to be one and just one, and in that one, I want to be able, to some degree, to recognize nature, be it nature that is tortured, because it involves a sort of battle between my internal life and the external world as it exists for most people. I have often said: I don't try to express nature, but to work like it. And I want to see this internal energy – my creative dynamics – presented to the person who looks at my paintings from the perspective of a violation of traditional painting."

▲ **Pablo Picasso** (1881-1973)
Women at the Fountain

▲ **Pablo Picasso** (1881-1973)
Woman in a White Hat
1920-1921

▶ **Pablo Picasso** (1881-1973)
Large Still Life
1917-1918

◀ **Pablo Picasso** (1881-1973)
Woman with Tambourine
1925

▲ **Henri Matisse** (1869-1954)
Draped Nude Lying Down
1923-1924

▲ **Henri Matisse** (1869-1954)
Three Sisters
1916-1917

▲ **Henri Matisse** (1869-1954)
Woman with a Violin
1921-1923

▲ **Henri Matisse** (1869-1954)
Odalisque in Gray Shorts
1927

Henri Matisse (1869-1954)
Odalisque in Red Pants
1924-1925

Henri Matisse (1869-1954) ▼
The Pink Nude or
the Young Girl with a Vase
of Flowers
1921

Henri Matisse (1869-1954) ▼
Blue Odalisque
or the White Slave
1921-1923

Henri Matisse (1869-1954) ▲
The Boudoir
1921

MATISSE: ADVICE TO A FUTURE PAINTER

Towards the end of his life, Henri Matisse, conscious of the feeling of apparent ease his paintings and sketches caused, wondered to what degree his influence would be damaging to young painters. He wrote: "I have always tried to hide my efforts. I have always hoped that my work would have the lightness and joy of spring that never lets you see the work required ... A future painter must discover what is useful to his own development — drawings and even sculpture — anything that will allow him to become one with Nature, to identify with her and delve into objects — that is what I call Nature — that which stimulates the senses. I think that sketching, as a study, is absolutely crucial. If a sketch precedes the Spirit and the color of the senses, one must sketch to cultivate the Spirit and be able to lead color through spiritual paths ... It is only after years of preparation that the young artist is entitled to handle colors — not colors as a means to describe — but as a means of intimate expression. Then he may hope that all of the images and even the symbols he uses might reflect his love for things, a reflection in which he can be confident ... Only then, he will use colors with discernment. He will place them according to a natural sketch, unformulated and fully conceived, that will rise straight up from his senses. This allowed Toulouse-Lautrec to exclaim at the end of his career: 'At last, I no longer know how to draw'."

Henri Matisse (1869-1954)
Woman on a Sofa
or the Divan
1921

DERAIN

The artistic career of the painter, drawer and sculptor, André Derain (1880-1954) was chaotic and contradictory, but captivating. Already in 1902, he declared: "Doctrines have advised us to be of our times; but that is complicated and, in doubt, I would rather say that we should be of all times." After having abandoned Fauvism (referred to as such because of the strident colors used by its followers), Derain remained one of the leaders of the avant-garde movement for a number of years. However, he increasingly believed that to "be of all times", he needed to reconcile with the timeless art of museums and tradition. Like few 20th century artists, he was convinced that all art from the past captures our visual universe, sometimes with nostalgia. Derain then moved towards Mannerism, painted more dutifully, and stretched bodies and faces to give them a more "gothic" appearance. He delved into Byzantine and Negro art, which he was one of the first to explore, and took inspiration from the painters of Pompeii and models such as Raphaël, Poussin, Caravaggio and Corot. He questioned them and transposed them with some casualness, purposefully awkward, creating a picture that was often apathetic, so as not to appear erudite. One can sense the search for a grand style supported by masterful techniques, yet devoid of passion. Did this return to the past express a loss of power? Surely not. He certainly used it more than other artists, but, like any great artist, imposed his style on all of his models.

▲ **André Derain** (1880-1954)
Kitchen Table
1925

André Derain (1880-1954) ▲
Arlequin and Pierrot
1924

DERAIN: PAINTING FOR ANTIQUE DEALERS?

Turning towards the past and searching for new truths, André Derain drew many detractors. Vlaminck, with whom he had a dispute, declared: "Derain creates modern paintings for antique dealers in Versailles." Not everyone shared this point of view. The writer Francis Carco wrote: "Why then, at times, despite his powerful message, do some sad colleagues criticize Derain for the conventional perspective they pretend to discover in his works? I admit that it bothers me less than the careless-ness with which painters who are compared to him get away with circumventing difficulties ... The point is not to copy the Masters who count but, thanks to them, to discover a path and follow it, even if one causes mass confusion."

▲ André Derain (1880-1954)
Black Man with a Mandolin
Circa 1930

▲ André Derain (1880-1954)
The Painter's Niece, Seated
Circa 1931

▲ **André Derain** (1880-1954)
Blond Model
Circa 1924

▲ **André Derain** (1880-1954)
Handsome Model
1923

▲ **André Derain** (1880-1954)
Portrait of Madame Paul
Guillaume in a Large Hat
Circa 1928-1929

▲ **André Derain** (1880-1954)
The Painter's Niece
Circa 1931

▶ UTRILLO

Maurice Utrillo (1883-1955), a self-taught artist who rapidly became a remarkable drawer, was the son of Suzanne Valadon (1867-1938), a liberated woman with a tempestuous love life and one of the most important painters of the beginning of the 20th century. The Spanish art critic, Miguel Utrillo, gave him his name in 1891. Alcoholism and various detoxification treatments, that many zealous critics took great efforts to broadcast, should not draw a shadow over uninterrupted artistic activity and very abundant works that met with success starting in 1919.

Utrillo is not a naïf painter in the same sense as the Douanier Rousseau. No candid surprises, no scruples in terms of style, but a throbbing melancholia that emanates from the description of his favorite themes, the City of Paris and its suburbs (particularly the Montmartre area). No waterlilies or impressions of a rising sun, no bright and triumphant colors, but a limited pallet with highly varied effects; a solid composition, classic rigor and a sharp sense of balance in his presentation of the decor of this enormous city, its long streets, often covered in snow and deserted, its walls with the lizardly plaster, café signs, squares, the grand cathedrals arising from low, heavy and threatening skies. When he uses lighter and airier colors (greens, light blues), he no longer illustrates the bitter truth of reality, nor the pallid light of places where poor people live. The spectator faces a surprising duality: infinite sadness and universal sympathy.

▶ **Maurice Utrillo** (1883-1955)
Notre-Dame
Circa 1910

UTRILLO: SOLITUDE AND SILENCE

It has been said that Maurice Utrillo painted naturally, like one peels an orange. But this surprising "large, timid devil, with sparkling eyes" (Francis Carco), worked constantly, alone in his little room, often at the end of the day, on the large paintings that represent Paris or his dear Butte Montmartre. He expressed much of the sadness in his soul in the false elegance of the streets, houses and trees. "Utrillo's work", a critic noted in 1938, "leads us to the most deserted corners of the kingdom of solitude and silence. No friendship, no recourse and even no palpable peace in the frigid calm of things. [...] For Utrillo, it's always Sunday, a dull Sunday with the bells of Montmartre stridently echoing and the suburbs arising from their weekly boredom, becoming aware of their existence, where the deserted streets of small towns remain symbolic of eternal absence."

▲ **Maurice Utrillo** (1883-1955)
The Butte Pinson
Circa 1905-1907

▲ **Maurice Utrillo** (1883-1955)
Berlioz' House
1914

▲ **Maurice Utrillo** (1883-1955)
Town Hall with Flag
1924

▲ **Maurice Utrillo** (1883-1955)
Maison Bernot
1924

SOUTINE

The French painter of Lithuanian origin, Chaïm Soutine (1893-1943), lived a miserable and anxiety-ridden childhood in a country under the rule of the Tsar's Empire, where he only knew hunger and the humiliating hostility of an environment towards his vocation. Upon his arrival in Paris in 1913, he assiduously visited museums, mostly interested in Rembrandt and Courbet, and met his fellow countrymen, Marc Chagall and Jacques Lipchitz. He was never rid of his anxiety, even after conquering poverty: it runs as a thread throughout his works (portraits, still lifes, landscapes), a shattering image of his internal visions and his reality – which makes him seem like an Expressionist. The bodies of his characters, with their scared, stunned or sly expressions, are distorted; their stance is sickly. Soutine only painted dead animals, as in the series of paintings representing bloody carcasses, the *Bœuf Ecorché (Carcass of Beef)* (with an obvious reference to Rembrandt) and the *Volailles (Birds)*, feathered or half-feathered, hung to a side of a wall by their beak or feet. His landscapes (the source for which he discovered in the south of France at Céret and Cagnes between 1915 and 1919) seem victims of his seismic jolts, destroying houses, dissembling structures, agitating and twisting trees, while steep paths reach to the sky and then plunge into a void. Soutine's pallet of colors – violent and obsessive reds, bluish whites and nightly blues – soften his incurable desperation, however, as well as his inexorable cruelty.

▲ **Chaïm Soutine** (1893-1943)
Fallen Tree
Circa 1923-1924

▶ Chaïm Soutine (1893-1943)
Young Englishwoman
Circa 1934

SOUTINE'S TRAGEDY

Intensity: this word characterizes all of Soutine's works. His portraits often represent a dismembered body or a terrible, terrorizing distortion. The hands of these excessive, enormous characters are nervous and as eloquent as their faces: the skin is always too red, as if gnawed by an incurable disease. They also reveal a true personality and universal nature. Their suffering seems all the more real as the environment (which is often nothing more than a curtain), their clothing and familiar objects are simply anecdotes. One can see the sad love and gentle understanding of a man. Nature, also inherently violent: trees, skies and flowers distorted in chaotic scenes.

▼ **Chaïm Soutine** (1893-1943)
Garçon d'Etage
Circa 1927

▲ **Chaïm Soutine** (1893-1943)
Gladiolas
Circa 1919

▲ **Chaïm Soutine** (1893-1943)
Garçon d'Honneur
Circa 1924-1925

NOTES

▶ P. 21 : Marcel Proust, *Du côté de chez Swann*, dans *À la recherche du temps perdu*,
Paris, Pléiade, 1st edition (1954), p. 169.

▶ P. 36 : Jean Renoir, *Pierre-Auguste* [sic] *Renoir, mon père*,
Paris, Gallimard, coll. « Folio », 1981, p. 237-238.

▶ P. 44 : Paul Cézanne, *Correspondance*,
Paris, Grasset, 1995, p. 240-241.

▶ P. 50 : Guillaume Apollinaire, *Chroniques d'art 1902-1918*,
Paris, Gallimard, coll. « Folio essais », 1993, p. 207-208.

▶ P. 58 : *Picasso. Dessins et œuvres en couleurs*,
Bâle, Éditions Beyeler, s. d., p. 72.

▶ P. 65 : Henri Matisse, *Écrits et propos sur l'art*,
Paris, Hermann, coll. « Savoir », 1972, p. 312-314.

▶ P. 69 : Francis Carco, *L'Ami des peintres*,
Paris, Gallimard, 1953, p. 101-102.

▶ P. 74 : Gabriel-Joseph Gros, *Utrillo*,
Lausanne, Marguerat, 1947, p. 133-134.

Artlys Director: Denis Kilian
editorial and iconographic coordination: Karine Barou, Hervé Delemotte and Dominique Jaillet
graphic design and production: Juliane Cordes and Corinne Dury
production: Pierre Kegels
photogravure: Aramis

ISBN-10: 2-85495-289-8
ISBN-13: 978-285495-289-6

achevé d'imprimer le 20 août 2006
par Les Presses de Bretagne (Cesson-Sévigné)
dépôt légal: septembre 2006